Aug 16

The Water Cycle

Nancy Dickmann

Cavendish Square

New York

Published in 2016 by Cavendish Square Publishing, LLC
243 5th Avenue, Suite 136, New York, NY 10016

CPSIA Compliance Information: Batch #CW16CSQ

All websites were available and accurate when this book was sent to press.

Cataloging-in-Publication Data

Dickmann, Nancy.
The water cycle / by Nancy Dickmann.
p. cm. — (Earth figured out)
Includes index.
ISBN 978-1-5026-0860-4 (hardcover) ISBN 978-1-5026-0858-1 (paperback)
ISBN 978-1-5026-0861-1 (ebook)
1. Hydrologic cycle — Juvenile literature. 2. Water — Juvenile literature.
I. Dickmann, Nancy. II. Title.
GB848.D53 2016
551.48—d23

Produced for Cavendish Square by Calcium
Editors: Sarah Eason and Harriet McGregor
Designer: Paul Myerscough

The photographs in this book are used by permission and through the courtesy of:
Prasert Wongchindawest/Shutterstock.com, cover; Insides: Shutterstock: ArtMari 23b, BlurAZ 29t,
Richard Bowden 4–5, Hector Conesa 28–29, Anton Foltin 8–9, Stefano Garau 15t, Dave Head
24–25, HurleySB 10, Jefunne 19r, Kazoka 12–13, Andrei Kuzmik 6–7, LiliGraphie 16, Alberto
Loyo 25b, Nebojsa Markovic 18–19, Vladimir Melnikov 1, Nina B 23t, Dasha Petrenko 7b, Igor
Rogozhnikov 14–15, StevanZZ 22–23, Stjepann 11, Swa182 21, TTstudio 12b, Merkushev Vasiliy
5b, Christian Vinces 26–27, Nickolay Vinokurov 27r, Trudy Wilkerson 20, Khongkit Wiriyachan 17,
Pan Xunbin 9t.

Printed in the United States of America

Contents

What Is the Water Cycle?

All living things rely on water. About three-quarters of your own body is made of water! Our planet is home to vast oceans of water, but nearly all of it is salty, meaning that we cannot drink it. Plants and animals rely on the **freshwater** that falls as rain and collects in rivers and lakes.

All the water on Earth—both freshwater and saltwater—is constantly recycled in a process called the water cycle. When water is heated, it turns into a gas and rises into the air. There, it collects in clouds, then cools, and turns back into liquid water. It falls back to Earth and eventually **evaporates** again.

EARTH FIGURED OUT

The amount of water on Earth has been about the same for millions of years. Earth's water is recycled over and over through the water cycle. In fact, the water you drink today may be the same water that a dinosaur drank more than 100 million years ago! Since then, it has probably evaporated and then fallen as **precipitation** millions of times.

The water cycle
is easy to figure out.
It has four steps:

Precipitation:
Water falls from the
sky as rain, snow,
sleet, or **hail**.

Condensation:
Water vapor collects
in clouds. As it cools,
it becomes liquid
water again.

Collection:
The land, streams,
rivers, oceans, lakes,
and other areas collect
the water that falls.

Evaporation:
Heat from the sun
causes water on
Earth to evaporate
and rise into the sky
as **water vapor**.

This diagram shows the four
steps of the water cycle.

Evaporation

A lot of water exists on Earth's surface. The oceans cover more than two-thirds of the planet, and even the large areas of land are home to rivers, lakes, and streams. The water in the oceans is salty, though the water on land is not. Any of Earth's water, either fresh or salty, can evaporate as part of the water cycle. The water turns into water vapor and rises into the air.

Like all substances, water is made up of tiny particles called **molecules**. They are too small to see, even with a microscope! Every molecule is constantly moving, and the warmer each molecule becomes, the faster it moves. Molecules often bump into other molecules, which gives them more energy. Once a water molecule near the surface has enough energy, it escapes into the air. This is evaporation.

When water boils to make steam, it is changing from a liquid to a gas—evaporation in action!

EARTH FIGURED OUT

Like most other substances, water can exist as a solid, a liquid, or a gas. The particles in a solid, such as ice, are tightly packed and cannot move very much. The particles in a liquid are less tightly packed, and they can move around more freely. The particles in a gas, such as water vapor, are loose and widely spaced. They move a lot, constantly bumping into each other.

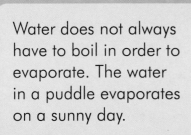

Water does not always have to boil in order to evaporate. The water in a puddle evaporates on a sunny day.

Transpiration

Not all of the water vapor in the air comes from oceans and lakes. Some water vapor is produced by plants in a process called **transpiration**. Most plants send **roots** down into the ground. These roots suck up moisture from the soil, and tiny tubes inside the plant carry the water to all its parts, including the leaves.

The undersides of a plant's leaves are covered with tiny holes called **stomata**. These holes release water in the form of water vapor. The water vapor escapes into the air. Transpiration in plants is a little like a person sweating, but when a plant is transpiring, its leaves do not feel wet. Plants transpire more in warm weather, when the sky is bright, or when it is windy. They transpire less when the air is humid. Around 10 percent of the moisture found in air comes from transpiration. The remaining 90 percent comes from evaporation.

Not all plants transpire at the same rate. Cacti do not transpire very much because they live in dry areas and need to keep hold of water.

EARTH FIGURED OUT

One reason that plants transpire is that it helps cool them down, in the same way that sweating cools a person. Transpiration also helps plants take in more **nutrients**. When a plant loses water though transpiration, its roots suck up more water from the soil. This water contains important nutrients.

The stomata in a plant's leaves allow water vapor to escape. They also allow the leaf to take in gases that the plant needs.

stomata

WATER—FIGURED OUT!

Earth has
332.5 billion
cubic miles (1.4 trillion cubic kilometers) of water. Water covers around 70 percent of Earth's surface. Ice, **icecaps**, and permanent snow make up 5.7 million cubic miles (24 million cubic km) of water.

The United States use about
355 billion
gallons (1.3 trillion Liters) of freshwater every day.

Water boils, or turns into a gas, at
212°
Fahrenheit (100° Celsius). However, water can evaporate at much lower temperatures, even at room temperature.

Most of Earth's freshwater—69 percent—is frozen in **glaciers** and icecaps. Just over 1 percent is found as liquid water at the surface, and about 21 percent of this amount is found in lakes. Rivers and lakes combined provide us with

22,300

cubic miles (92,950 cubic km) of freshwater.

In one year, a large oak tree can release

40,000

gallons (151,416 L) of water vapor through transpiration.

30

percent of all freshwater comes from beneath the ground. The water soaks into the ground deep below Earth's surface and resurfaces at springs.

Condensation

Water vapor in the air does not always stay as a gas. The higher you go, the cooler the air becomes. Cold air cools down the rising water vapor. When it gets cold enough, it turns back into a liquid. This is called **condensation**. It is the reverse of evaporation.

You can see condensation when you breathe warm air onto a mirror or window. Tiny water droplets form on the glass and make it look cloudy. The water vapor in your breath is cooled as it comes into contact with the cold glass, and it condenses into tiny droplets.

When water vapor in the air condenses, it can take several different forms. The dew you see on grass on a fall morning is a type of condensation. It is caused when water vapor comes into contact with cold ground. Fog and mist are also types of condensation.

Fog and mist often form at night, when the temperature falls. They disappear in the warmth of the day.

When you pour a cold drink, tiny water droplets soon form on the outside of the glass. Water vapor in the air condenses when it hits the cold glass.

EARTH FIGURED OUT

Warm air is lighter than cool air. This is because its molecules are more spaced out. When the ground is heated by sunshine, it warms up. This causes the air just above it to become warmer, too. The warmed air rises because it is lighter than the air around it.

Clouds

Even on a cloudless day, the air is still full of water vapor—you just can't see it. However, when water condenses high in the sky, it forms clouds. Clouds are masses of water droplets in the air. The water droplets are so small and light that they are able to stay in the air instead of falling to Earth.

We've already seen that cool air can cause condensation. Condensation can also happen when a mass of air becomes **saturated**. This means that it contains so much water vapor that it cannot hold any more. The molecules of water vapor are pressed closer together, and they eventually form droplets.

Water vapor condenses more easily when it has something to stick to. It can condense on small particles of dust, pollen, or other substances in the air. When tiny water droplets bump into each other, they stick together, and eventually form a cloud.

EARTH FIGURED OUT

There are many different types of clouds. Cirrus clouds are thin, wispy clouds found high in the sky. Stratus clouds are low, flat clouds. Cumulus clouds are low-lying clouds with a thick, puffy shape.

Cumulonimbus clouds (sometimes called thunderclouds) are heavy and dense. They can cause heavy rain, hailstorms, or tornadoes.

High, wispy cirrus clouds are bright white during the day, but they can also take on the colors of the sunset.

CONDENSATION—FIGURED OUT!

An average-sized cloud can weigh about

875,000 pounds

(400,000 kilograms), which is as much as a fully-loaded 747 airplane! A really big cumulonimbus cloud can be 10,000 times heavier. Because this weight is spread out over a huge area, the cloud can stay airborne.

The water droplets in a cloud can be far smaller than the period at the end of this sentence, at just

0.0004 inches

(0.01 millimeters) long. The largest droplets are about 0.2 inches (5 mm) across.

The bottom of a cumulus cloud might be only 1,200 feet (365 meters) above the ground, while a cirrus cloud floats at about

40,000 feet

(12,192 m) above the ground.

The highest a passenger jet normally flies is about **39,000** feet (almost 11,900 m). At this altitude, it will be above nearly all the clouds in the sky.

The water droplets in a cloud are so tiny that nearly **3 million** of them fit into each cubic foot (28 L) of air.

A towering cumulonimbus cloud can reach more than **12** miles (19 km) up into the sky, and it can weigh up to 1 million tons (907,185 metric tons).

Precipitation

Precipitation is any form of water falling from the sky, and it is probably the easiest part of the water cycle to see in action. The most common type of precipitation is rain, but there are many other types, including sleet, snow, hail, and drizzle. Some types of precipitation, such as rain, are liquid water. Other types, such as hail, are solid ice.

Many clouds never release any precipitation. Warm air rising from the ground helps to push a cloud up and keep it in the air. The droplets of water in the cloud are often too small and light to overcome these **updrafts** and fall to the ground.

However, sometimes the droplets grow big and heavy enough to fall from the cloud as rain. This often happens when they bump into each other and clump together. Snow forms in a similar way: water droplets freeze into tiny **ice crystals** and stick together to form snowflakes.

EARTH FIGURED OUT

A lot of the water in clouds comes from water that has evaporated from the salty oceans. So why isn't rain salty?

The answer is that when water from the oceans evaporates, the salt is left behind. Only pure water forms clouds.

When the temperature is cold, precipitation can fall as sleet, snow, or freezing rain.

When ice crystals clump together to form snowflakes, they often form beautiful patterns.

FALLING WATER—FIGURED OUT!

It can take more than

1 million

water droplets to make a
single raindrop.

Mount Waialeale in Hawaii
holds the record for the highest
average yearly rainfall:

37.5 feet (11 m)

per year. However, the rainiest
year ever recorded was in
Cherrapunji, India, in 1861, when
75.4 feet (23 m) of rain fell!

The ice crystals that form
snow take up more space than
liquid water. Depending on the
temperature during the snowstorm,

13 inches (33 cm)

of snow on the ground contains the
same amount of water as
1 inch (2.5 cm) of rain.

Most hailstones are less than

1
inch (2.5 cm) across, but the largest can be up to 6 inches (15 cm) in diameter!

If all the precipitation that fell on the forty-eight states of the US mainland stayed on the surface, it would cover the entire area to a depth of

30
inches (76 cm).

During a heavy rainstorm, the average raindrop will be about

0.1
inch (0.25 cm) across and will fall at a speed of 22 feet (7 m) per second. If you marked out an area of 1 square foot (0.1 square meter), approximately forty-six drops will fall on it each second.

Collection

When precipitation falls to the ground, it has to go somewhere. This stage of the water cycle is often known as **collection**, and it can take many forms. For example, a lot of rain falls directly on the oceans, where it can eventually evaporate again.

When rain falls on the land, a small amount lands in rivers, streams, or lakes, but most of it soaks into the ground. It might eventually enter a stream, or it might go deeper into the ground. Some of this underground water returns to the surface when an **aquifer** empties into a lake or river.

When snow falls in cold climates, it is often stored on the surface. In some places, enough snow builds up to form glaciers and icecaps. Some of this frozen water will eventually melt and flow into rivers.

When rain falls, a lot of it seeps deep underground, where it is collected in an aquifer.

EARTH FIGURED OUT

An aquifer is a layer of rock deep underground that can store water. The type of rock in an aquifer has small openings that liquids and gases can pass through.

When water seeps into the ground, it often ends up in an aquifer, where it can be stored. People drill wells to reach the water in aquifers.

Glaciers flow very slowly down to the sea, where enormous chunks of ice often break off to form icebergs.

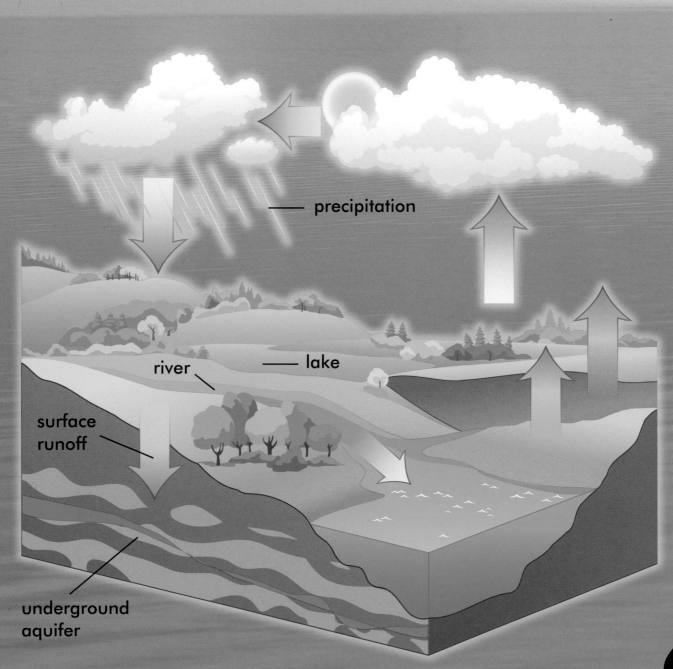

precipitation

river

lake

surface runoff

underground aquifer

Surface Runoff

Some water that falls on land flows back to the oceans, in a process called surface runoff. It happens when rain falls on land that cannot soak up water. This might be because the rocks are too hard to soak up water, or because the ground already holds as much water as it can.

Flowing water always moves downhill. After a heavy rainstorm, you might see water near the curb flowing down the street. The same thing happens in the wilderness, where surface water moves from higher ground to lower ground. As the water trickles down, it collects in small channels that join together to make larger ones. These channels have many different names: creeks, brooks, cricks, streams, or rivulets, for example. As the water moves downhill, the streams eventually join a larger river and flow down to the ocean or sea.

Many rivers enter the ocean at an estuary, where freshwater and saltwater mix. Estuaries are important habitats for wildlife.

EARTH FIGURED OUT

A lot ot the salt in the oceans actually comes from rocks on land. As water flows over land, it breaks down rocks. These rocks contain many different chemicals, including salts. Some of these chemicals are carried by streams and rivers, all the way to the oceans.

Runoff can also occur when snow melts. For example, the snowcap at the top of a mountain may melt in the spring, and this water feeds fast-flowing mountain streams.

COLLECTION—FIGURED OUT!

Around **1/3** of the precipitation that falls on land returns to rivers and oceans. The other two-thirds either soak into the ground or evaporate back into the air.

The largest aquifer ever discovered is in Australia. It covers **661,000** square miles (1.7 million sq km), which is around 22 percent of the entire country. Scientists estimate that it contains 15,600 cubic miles (65,000 cubic km) of groundwater.

Some water has a very long journey back to the sea. From the source of the Nile River, water must travel **4,132** miles (6,650 km) to reach the Mediterranean Sea.

Of all Earth's rivers, the mighty Amazon releases the most water. Every second it releases more than **6 million** cubic feet (169,900 cubic m) into the Atlantic Ocean! The Amazon is the source of approximately 20 percent of all the freshwater released by rivers into the oceans.

On average, around **3.5** percent of the oceans is made up of salt. Some lakes and seas are much saltier, though. The Dead Sea, in the Middle East, is one of Earth's saltiest bodies of water. It is made up of about 34 percent salt.

We Need the Water Cycle

Once water flows down a river and returns to the ocean, it can evaporate, starting the cycle over. Some water might stay trapped in a glacier or underground aquifer for a long time—maybe even thousands of years. Other water might be drunk or used to water crops before evaporating or transpiring again. The water cycle is a complicated process!

If we didn't have the water cycle, life on Earth would be extremely difficult. We depend on precipitation for the water that makes plants grow. If there was no rain, farmers could still get water from **wells** to water their crops—at least until the aquifers dried up—but huge areas of forest would die unless they were watered. Rivers and lakes would eventually dry out, either by evaporating or emptying into the oceans. Without doubt, we need the water cycle!

EARTH FIGURED OUT

Humans can affect the water cycle in a number of ways. For example, we build **dams** that trap water in rivers, keeping it from flowing back to the ocean. We use wells to take water from underground aquifers. We even spray chemicals into clouds that help make rain fall. Some of these actions can harm the environment.

A rainstorm can spoil your day, but the rain is incredibly important. Without it, life on Earth could not exist!

We can't live without freshwater, so it is important not to waste this natural resource.

Glossary

aquifer A layer of rock, sand, or gravel underground that contains water.

collection The stage in the water cycle where precipitation is gathered after it falls, either on the surface or underground.

condensation The process of changing from a gas to a liquid.

dams Structures, such as walls, built across rivers or streams to keep them from flowing.

evaporates When water turns from a liquid into a gas.

freshwater Water that is not salty.

glaciers Large masses of ice that move very slowly down slopes or across land.

hail Small, round pieces of ice that fall from the sky.

icecaps Large, thick sheets of ice that spread out over the land.

ice crystals Shapes formed when water freezes in regular shapes.

molecules The smallest units of a substance that have all the properties of that substance.

nutrients Substances that help humans, animals, and plants to live and grow.

precipitation Water that falls from the sky as rain, snow, sleet, or hail.

roots The parts of a plant that suck up water and nutrients from the soil.

saturated Not able to hold any more water.

stomata Tiny holes on the underside of a plant's leaf that allow water and gases to move in and out.

transpiration The process by which a plant releases water vapor from its leaves into the air.

updrafts Currents of air that are moving upward.

water vapor Water that is in the form of gas.

wells Deep holes dug in the ground to reach water or other resources.

Further Reading

Books

Dakers, Diane. *Earth's Water Cycle.* Earth's Cycles in Action. New York: Crabtree Publishing Company, 2014.

Duke, Shirley. *Step-By-Step Experiments with the Water Cycle.* North Mankato, MN: Child's World, 2012.

Hutmacher, Kimberly. *The Wonderful Water Cycle.* My Science Library. Vero Beach, FL: Rourke Publishing, 2012.

Morgan, Sally. *The Water Cycle.* Nature's Cycles. New York: Rosen Publishing Group, 2009.

Ransom, Candice. *Investigating the Water Cycle.* Searchlight Books. Minneapolis, MN: Lerner Publishing, 2015.

Websites

At this site you can learn more about the different types of precipitation:
education.nationalgeographic.com/education/encyclopedia/precipitation/?ar_a=1

Visit this site to learn more about the water cycle, including photos of different types of clouds:
eo.ucar.edu/kids/green/cycles3.htm

Find out more about clouds, including a cloud identification quiz, at:
scied.ucar.edu/webweather/clouds

This site has lots of useful information about water and the water cycle, as well as activities and a water glossary:
water.usgs.gov/edu/index.html

Index